Great Hikes of
Rocky Mountain
National Park

by Dav[...]

Book and Cover Design by Jonathan Norberg

Photos: Front cover of Longs Peak from the trail to Lake Haiyaha;
  back cover by Jeff Wendland; all others by the author

Maps provided by mytopo.com

10 9 8 7 6 5 4 3 2 1

Copyright 2013 by Dave Marriner
Published by Adventure Publications, Inc.
820 Cleveland Street South
Cambridge, Minnesota 55008
1-800-678-7006
www.adventurepublications.net
Printed in China
ISBN: 978-1-59193-420-2

Table of Contents

INTRODUCTION

Rocky Mountain National Park is a showcase for the Rocky Mountains. One of the country's natural treasures, the park is home to jagged peaks, alpine lakes, pristine meadows, crashing waterfalls, barren tundra and a plethora of wildlife. The purpose of this book is to help you make the most of your time in the park by helping you choose the best hikes for you. These 12 trails provide an excellent cross-section of the hiking options at the park; they range in difficulty and each has something very special to offer. When exploring Rocky Mountain National Park, there are a number of things to take into account:

WEATHER—Conditions can change quickly in the park and what starts out as a mild sunny day can turn to snow or a storm by afternoon. Particularly above timberline, lightning can be a real danger in the summer, when afternoon thunderstorms are common. If a storm is brewing, start your adventures earlier in the day. Check the ranger station for the weather report and be sure you're equipped with the necessary apparel for your outing.

WILDLIFE—From chipmunks and birds to moose, bears and mountain lions, the park is home to wild animals of all shapes and sizes. Do not feed, approach or harass the wildlife. Enjoy them from afar and take as many pictures as you like.

ALTITUDE—The lowest spot in the park is well above 7000 feet and the air only gets thinner from there. If you come from a lower elevation, take time to acclimate to the altitude. Dizziness, nausea or shortness of breath can all be symptoms of altitude sickness, which can be a serious problem. If you suspect you're suffering from it, get medical help.

GO PREPARED—Be sure you are well equipped: stay hydrated, know your limits, protect yourself from the sun (UV rays are intense at these altitudes), and bring all the gear you'll need.

LEAVE NO TRACE—If you take something in, be sure to bring it out as well. So that future generations can enjoy this national treasure, leave the park as undisturbed as possible.

TRAIL SURFACE—The trails in the book are typically packed dirt and natural rock. Some are better maintained than others and some have more rock than packed dirt but the rocks are usually not loose. Most of the trails are roughly 4 to 6 feet wide, though some trails, such as the Tombstone Ridge Trail, are narrower.

DIFFICULTY—A hike's level of difficulty can be subjective but all of these trails involve some level of fitness. Before you set out, note the length and altitude change.

PARK RULES—No pets, bikes or motor vehicles of any kind are allowed on the park trails. Some trails do allow horses and since some trails interconnect, it's important to check with park officials for clarification before bringing horses onto any trail.

PARK CONTACT INFORMATION:
Phone: 970-586-1206
Website: www.nps.gov/romo
Mail: Rocky Mountain National Park, 1000 Highway 36, Estes Park, CO, 80517-8397

OVERVIEW MAP

HIKES
1. Ouzel Falls
2. Emerald Lake
3. Lake Haiyaha
4. The Loch
5. Odessa Lake
6. Twin Owls
7. Gem Lake
8. Tombstone Ridge
9. Forest Canyon Pass
10. Granite Falls
11. Cascade Falls
12. East Meadow

Water is the main attraction in this adventure. The highlights of the hike are Ouzel Falls and Calypso Cascades, but the thundering mountain streams nearby keep this route constantly interesting. There are numerous spots where you can sit on a sunny rock by the creek and take in the power of the water that rushes by.

Location

From Estes Park, take Hwy. 7 south for about 13 miles to Wild Basin Road. Turn right (west) on Wild Basin Road and then turn right into the Copeland Lake area. Follow the dirt road until it terminates at the Wild Basin Trailhead in a little over 2 miles. The trail begins on the south side of the parking area.

LEFT: Morning daylight on Ouzel Falls

Trail Details

After just over a quarter mile from the trailhead you will come to a side trail on the left, which leads to Copeland Falls. Calling this a waterfall may be a bit generous, but it is a great spot to watch the water cutting its way through the rock. For about the next 1.5 miles, the rushing water is always nearby. As the trail steepens, the path of the water crashes over boulders, and this reaches a pinnacle at Calypso Cascades. There, the trail leaves the drainage and heads higher toward Ouzel Falls. When you reach the falls, work your way up the left bank of the creek to view one of the best waterfalls in the park. Return the way you came.

Other Info

- One-way distance: Copeland Falls, 0.3 miles, Calypso Cascades, 1.8 miles, Ouzel Falls, 2.7 miles

- Elevation change is 950 feet to Ouzel Falls

- Trailhead is busy; arrive early for a good parking spot

- Pit toilets are located at the trailhead

The Emerald Lake Trail is the quintessential mountain lake hike. This reasonably short trail passes both Nymph and Dream Lakes on the way to the final destination of Emerald Lake. Each lake has its own unique character and views that never end. If you're feeling ambitious you can also add Lake Haiyaha (see page 16) to the outing for a longer adventure.

Location

Take US Hwy. 36 from Estes Park to the Beaver Meadows Entrance to RMNP. Travel 0.2 miles past the entrance and turn left on Bear Lake Rd. After about 8.5 miles you'll arrive at the Bear Lake Trailhead at the end of the road, where the route begins. The park's shuttle service also stops here.

LEFT: Dream Lake on the way to Emerald Lake

Trail Details

Signs at the trailhead direct you to Emerald Lake.
The trail starts with a gradual half-mile incline that
passes through a forest and leads to Nymph Lake.
Continue around the right side of the lake, and it
begins to climb again and passes some nice rock
outcroppings and panoramic views of Longs Peak.
As you approach Dream Lake, there's a fork in the
trail. Take a right; you'll arrive at Dream Lake almost
immediately. This is an absolutely gorgeous lake,
so take it all in. To continue to Emerald Lake, travel
around the right side of Dream Lake. The path winds
through boulders; you'll see the lake once you crest
the hill. Return the way you came.

Other Info

- One-way distance: Nymph Lake, 0.5 miles, Dream
  Lake, 1.1 miles, Emerald Lake, 1.8 miles; combine
  with Lake Haiyaha (page 16) for more exploring

- Elevation change is 605 feet to Emerald Lake

- A busy trailhead; arrive early or take the park shuttle;
  pit toilets are at the trailhead

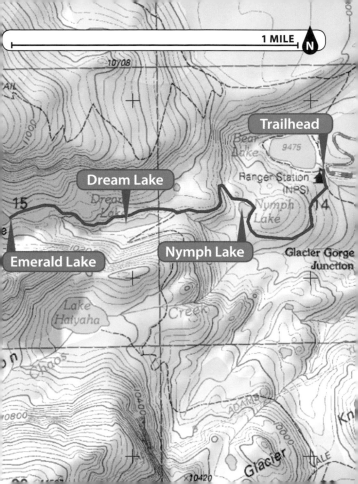

The path to Lake Haiyaha offers some of the most incredible views of Longs Peak. The crystal clear water of the lake is surrounded by a gigantic boulder field that is fun to negotiate and scramble across. Find a nearby rock, have a seat, and let your senses take it all in.

Location

Take US Hwy. 36 from Estes Park to the Beaver Meadows Entrance to RMNP. Travel 0.2 miles past the entrance and turn left on Bear Lake Rd. After about 8.5 miles you will arrive at the Bear Lake Trailhead at the end of the road. This is where the hike starts. The park also provides a shuttle service that stops at this location.

Trail Details

The first mile of this trail actually overlaps the Emerald Lake Trail (page 12) so start off by finding the signs that direct you to Emerald Lake. You will pass Nymph Lake on the way, and about 0.5 miles later, as you approach Dream Lake, there will be a fork in the trail. Take a left toward Lake Haiyaha but check out Dream Lake first. The trail rises quickly through dense forest before it levels out, offering stellar views of Longs Peak. At the next intersection take a right and approach the lake. The final section involves a bit of route-finding across rocks. Return the way you came.

Other Info

- One-way distance: Nymph Lake 0.5 miles, Dream Lake 1.1 miles, Lake Haiyaha 2.1 miles; combine with Emerald Lake (page 12) for a longer outing

- Elevation change is 745 feet to Lake Haiyaha

- Busy trailhead, so arrive early or take the park shuttle; pit toilets are at the trailhead

This is a journey to The Loch, a subalpine lake that soothes the soul. The Loch is a perfect mix of water, rock, trees and towering mountains. Along the way you will pass Alberta Falls, which is a destination in its own right. Much of this hike is paralleled by rushing water, a perfect soundtrack to the breathtaking views.

Location

Take US Hwy. 36 from Estes Park to the Beaver Meadows Entrance to RMNP. Travel 0.2 miles past the entrance and turn left on Bear Lake Rd. Go about 7.5 miles to the Glacier Gorge trailhead on the left. The trail starts here. The park also provides a shuttle service to this location.

Trail Details

The trail is well marked; just follow the signs to Loch Vale. The well-maintained path follows a creek then cuts left through a forest that has as many boulders as trees. This leads to Glacier Gorge, which the trail then parallels until you come upon Alberta Falls. As you head away from the falls, the route gets steeper and the views begin to emerge. The closer you get to The Loch, the more impressive the views become. After a few final switchbacks you crest a hill to arrive at The Loch. The trail continues on to other lakes, but head left. Here, you'll find a great place to relax and soak it all in. Return the way you came.

Other Info

- One-way distance: Alberta Falls, 0.8 miles, The Loch, 3.1 miles

- Elevation change is 990 feet to The Loch

- Busy trailhead so arrive early or take the park shuttle

- Pit toilets are at the trailhead

5 Odessa Lake

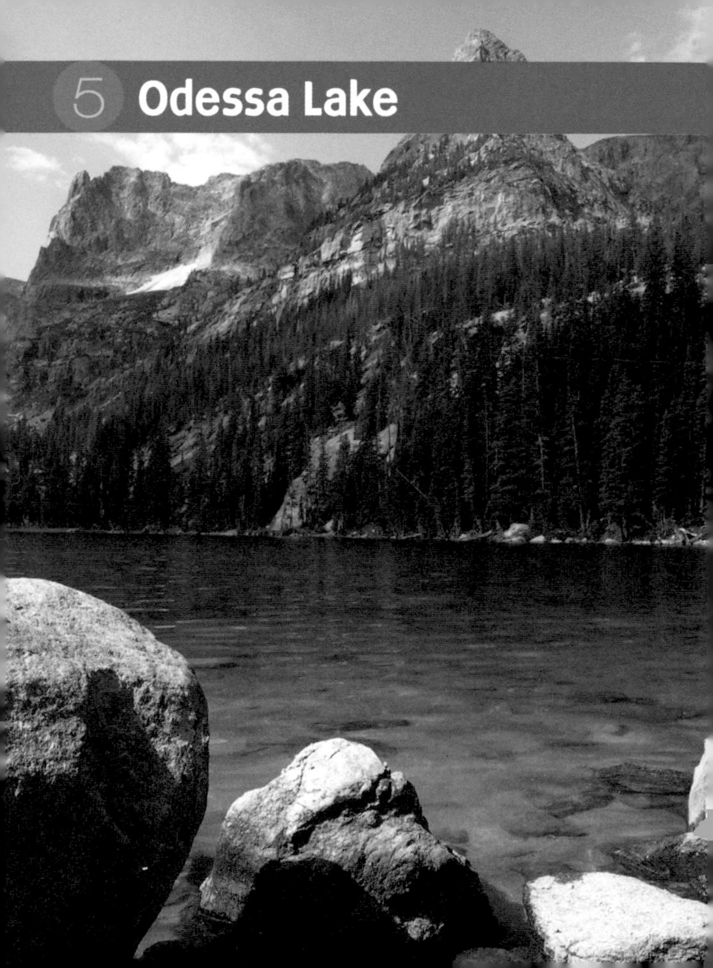

If you're looking for a more challenging hike, try Odessa Lake. Surrounded by towering peaks, the lake's beauty is inspiring. Along the way you'll pass The Pool, Fern Falls and Fern Lake, all destinations in their own right. When combined with Odessa Lake, they make a superb way to spend the better part of a day.

Location

Take US Hwy. 36 from Estes Park to the Beaver Meadows Entrance to RMNP. Travel 0.2 miles past the entrance and turn left on Bear Lake Rd. After about 1.25 miles take a right toward Fern Lake Trailhead and Moraine Park Campground. Take a left just before the campground. The road ends in 2 miles at Fern Lake Trailhead. The park's shuttle stop is 0.8 miles before the trailhead.

LEFT: Odessa Lake

Trail Details

For the first 1.7 miles, the trail is fairly level as it parallels the Big Thompson River and leads to The Pool. Once you cross the bridge at The Pool, take the path to the right and prepare for the ascent. From here, the trail is consistently steep, but there are several great sights to distract you. The first is Fern Falls, which is located at a switchback in the trail, about 0.7 miles past The Pool. Roughly 1.5 miles past the falls, you'll arrive at Fern Lake. Enjoy the serenity of this location, then continue around the left side of the lake; after another 0.7 miles, you'll reach Odessa Lake and be rewarded for your efforts. Enjoy the downhill walk back.

Other Info

- One-way distance: The Pool, 1.7 miles, Fern Falls, 2.4 miles, Fern Lake, 3.8 miles, Odessa Lake, 4.6 miles

- Elevation change is 1855 feet to Odessa Lake

- Parking is limited, so arrive early or take the shuttle and walk the 0.8 miles to the trailhead; pit toilets are located at the shuttle stop, but not the trailhead

Trailhead

The Pool

Fern Falls

Fern Lake

Odessa Lake

1 MILE

N

The Twin Owls Loop leads you through a ponderosa pine and spruce forest filled with interesting rock outcroppings. The Twin Owls is an enormous monolith that towers above for nearly the entire time. In addition to the nice views of Longs Peak and the Continental Divide, most of the trail provides good solitude.

Location

From Estes Park take the US Hwy. 34 bypass past the Stanley Hotel. After the Stanley Hotel, turn right (north) on MacGregor Ave. Once on MacGregor it will curve sharply to the right and turn into Devil's Gulch Rd. About 0.75 miles later, turn left on Lumpy Ridge Rd. The trailhead is at the end of the road.

LEFT: The Twin Owls towering above

Trail Details

At the trailhead, take the path to the left toward Twin Owls and the Black Canyon Trail. The path starts by climbing over a ridge and down the other side with great views of the Twin Owls and other rock formations. The path continues through a spruce, aspen and ponderosa pine forest; views of Longs Peak and the Continental Divide dominate the south. Take a right at the first intersection toward the Gem Lake Trail. The route passes below the Twin Owls and soon connects with the Gem Lake Trail. Turn right onto the Gem Lake Trail and walk down a pretty draw with nice outcroppings. This path leads back to the trailhead.

Other Info

- Total distance is 1.6 miles

- Elevation change is 310 ft.

- Pit toilets are at the trailhead

- Can be combined with Gem Lake (page 32) for a more involved adventure

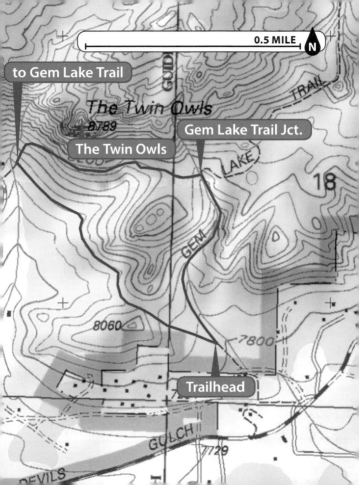

0.5 MILE N

to Gem Lake Trail

The Twin Owls
8789

Gem Lake Trail Jct.

The Twin Owls

LAKE TRAIL

GUID

GEM LAKE

18

8060

7800

Trailhead

GULCH

729

DEVILS

Although Gem Lake is a great destination by itself, it's the journey there that makes this adventure so exceptional. This steep trail constantly weaves through interesting rock formations and eventually takes you between, over and across the rocks themselves.

Location

From Estes Park take the US Hwy. 34 bypass past the Stanley Hotel. After the Stanley, turn right (north) on MacGregor Ave. Once on MacGregor it will curve sharply to the right and become Devil's Gulch Rd. About 0.75 miles later, turn left on Lumpy Ridge Rd. The trailhead is at the end of the road.

LEFT: Rock formations on the way to Gem Lake

Trail Details

At the trailhead, take the path to the right for Gem Lake. The trail ascends immediately, passing through a pretty draw with great rock outcroppings until it meets a side trail to the Twin Owls. From there, the path heads through a ponderosa pine and spruce forest, with more interesting rock formations, and eventually enters another drainage. The route becomes more enclosed as the cliffs rise above you and the trail starts to wind through, around and over the rock itself. The last part of the journey is the steepest as well as the most interesting, so pace yourself and enjoy. At the top of this incline you will arrive at Gem Lake. Return the way you came.

Other Info

- One-way distance: Gem Lake, 1.7 miles; for a longer hike, combine it with the Twin Owls hike (page 28)

- Elevation change is 950 ft.

- Pit toilets are at the trailhead and there is a privy just before Gem Lake

8 Tombstone Ridge

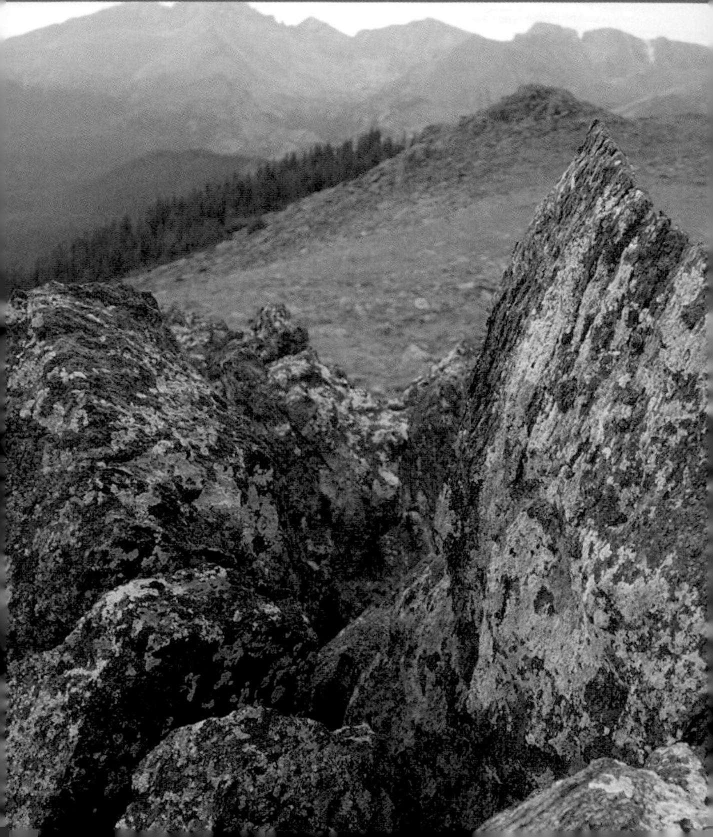

Trail Ridge Road is a great way to see the tundra from a distance, but Tombstone Ridge is the way to experience the tundra up-close. Here you can see the tundra's tiny flowers, colorful lichens and never-ending views. As you hike, be on the lookout for the marmots and pikas that call this place home.

Location

Take US Hwy. 36 from Estes Park to the Beaver Meadows Entrance to RMNP. Continue past the entrance for 13.4 miles up Trail Ridge Road. There is a pullout on the left that is the trailhead for the Ute Trail, where the hike begins.

LEFT: Lichen covered rocks on Tombstone Ridge

Trail Details

The ascent into the tundra begins as you leave the parking area. The views are great on this trail, and as the first mile of the trail ascends Tombstone Ridge, the scenery becomes even more impressive. The trail levels out a bit in the middle before descending down to Timberline Pass. There is no sign marking Timberline Pass, but it is easy to spot as the trail begins a much steeper descent at this point. This happens 2 miles from the trailhead and is an ideal spot to turn back. Return the way you came.

Other Info

- One-way distance: 2 miles

- Elevation change is 240 feet

- Trail Ridge Road is open seasonally, so the trailhead is only accessible Memorial Day to mid-October

- There are no toilets at the trailhead

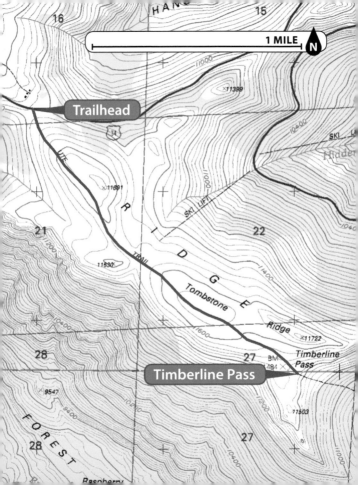

Forest Canyon Pass is another great way to explore the tundra. From the trailhead, the trail gradually descends until it passes through the stunted trees that somehow survive at timberline. Marmots and pikas are common and the views are exceptional. If you plan ahead and have access to a second vehicle, you can hike through to Milner Pass.

Location

Take US Hwy. 36 from Estes Park to the Beaver Meadows Entrance to RMNP. Continue on Hwy. 36 until it merges into US Hwy. 34 and heads up Trail Ridge Road. About 2 miles past the highest point on the road, you'll arrive at the Alpine Visitor Center. The trail begins just across Trail Ridge Road.

LEFT: A small pond near Forest Canyon Pass

Trail Details

From the parking lot, take the crosswalk across Trail Ridge Road to the very well-maintained trail on the other side. As with most trails above timberline, the views are great before you even leave the car. The path gradually descends from the visitor center and eventually reaches timberline. These stunted trees have survived in the harshest of environments and are intriguing to see. The trail continues to drop until you reach a few small ponds just before the pass. A little farther along there is a sign for Forest Canyon Pass. Return the way you came.

Other Info

- One-way distance: 2 miles

- Elevation change is -400 feet to Forest Canyon Pass

- Trail Ridge Road is open seasonally and the trailhead is only accessible Memorial Day to mid-October

- Toilets are available at the parking lot; if you plan ahead and have a second car, this mostly downhill hike could connect to Milner Pass (4.3 miles)

1 MILE   N

Trailhead

Forest Canyon Pass

Granite Falls carves and crashes its way over a huge granite slab and just begs to be enjoyed. It is the perfect place to relax while witnessing the power of nature before your eyes. At just over 10 miles round-trip, this is also the longest trek in this book and a great way to spend the better part of a day.

Location

Take US Hwy. 34 into the park from the Grand Lake (west) side. From the entrance gate, continue about 3 miles to the Green Mountain Trailhead, which is located on the right side of the road. The trail heads east out of the southern part of the parking lot.

LEFT: Granite Falls

Trail Details

From the parking lot, this trail heads into a dense forest, and a small stream is nearby. It climbs consistently for about the first 1.5 miles until it levels out and drops a bit to Big Meadows. At 1.8 miles the path begins to skirt around the left side of Big Meadows. Almost immediately you come across the remnants of some old cabins. After 1.2 miles of navigating around Big Meadows, the path begins to parallel Tonahutu Creek. For just over the last 2 miles, the sounds of the creek are always present as the trail steadily climbs its way to Granite Falls. Take some time to enjoy the falls and return the way you came.

Other Info

- One-way distance: Big Meadows 1.8 miles, Granite Falls, 5.2 miles

- The elevation change to Granite Falls is 1046 feet

- Pit toilets are present at the trailhead

1 MILE N

R O C K Y   M O U N T A I N

Old Cabins

Granite Falls

N A T I O N A L   F O R E S T

Trailhead

Cascade Falls is the thundering finale to a great adventure that ventures through peaceful meadows and a pleasant forest. This trail is interesting from the start and only becomes more dramatic as you approach the waterfall. With only 300 feet of elevation gain, this is also one of the easier trails in the park.

Location

From US Hwy. 34 on the west side of the park, take the only road heading into Grand Lake. In 0.2 miles take the left fork in the road and head toward the Adams Falls Trailhead. After another 0.9 miles turn left and follow the sign that directs you toward the North Inlet Trailhead. Continue up a hill and arrive at the trailhead.

LEFT: Cascade Falls

Trail Details

The trail actually begins at a blocked-off road and crosses private property. The grade is very easy and the scenery is excellent, but be sure to stay on the trail. In a little over a mile, the road narrows to a path and you leave private property. The route continues through a very pretty forest as the grade steadily increases. As you get closer to the falls, the cliffs and rock outcroppings start to become the predominant features. The final part of the trail takes you across a cutout section of the cliff. From here it's a short distance to the falls, but you'll hear the falls before you see them. Enjoy the surroundings and return the way you came.

Other Info

- One-way distance: 3.4 miles
- Elevation change is 300 feet
- Pit toilets are available at the trailhead

East Meadow is one of the better places to spot moose in the park, and the beautiful and serene setting makes it something special. This highly visited trail begins with Adams Falls, but the crowd thins as you continue a bit farther to East Meadow. Walk through a forest on the edge of the meadow with excellent views, and finish at a nice little bonus waterfall.

Location

From US Hwy. 34 on the west side of the park, take the only road heading into Grand Lake. In 0.2 miles take the left fork in the road heading toward the Adams Falls trailhead. After another 2 miles turn left into the Adams Falls trailhead. This is where the adventure begins.

Trail Details

Most people come here to see Adams Falls; to get there, hike 0.3 miles from the trailhead. There, you'll see a spur trail on the right. Remain on the spur trail after the falls, as it will lead back to the main path. You'll soon leave the crowds behind as you make your way to East Meadow. Here, the trail levels out and the views open up. The route skirts around the edge of a meadow and passes through the woods, but there are open areas to take in the scenery. As you near the end of the meadow, the path cuts into the forest and eventually comes to a nice side creek that has a small footbridge and a pretty waterfall. This "bonus" waterfall is a good place to turn around and head back. Be on the lookout for moose on your way out.

Other Info

- One-way distance: Adams Falls, 0.3 miles, footbridge at bonus waterfall, 2.1 miles

- Elevation change is 246 feet

- Pit toilets are at the trailhead